ilka Michel · SUITE HOME CHICAGO

ilka Michel

SUITE HOME CHICAGO

An International Exhibition of Urban Street Furniture

Photography: ilka Michel
Text: Deborah Wilk

NEPTUN VERLAG

City of Chicago
Richard M. Daley, Mayor

Chicago Department of Cultural Affairs
Lois Weisberg, Commissioner

Chicago Department of Cultural Affairs
78 E. Washington St.
Chicago, Illinois 60602
312.744.6630
tty: 312.744.2947
www.cityofchicago.org/CulturalAffairs/

Erlenstrasse 2, CH-8280 Kreuzlingen
neptun@bluewin.ch
www.neptunart.ch

Design, Setting:
Roland Kaufmann, Logotype, CH-8272 Ermatingen

Photography: ilka Michel

Text: Deborah Wilk

ISBN 3-85820-153-7

Message from the Mayor

Dear Friends:

As Mayor and on behalf of the City of Chicago, thank you for your support of *Suite Home Chicago*®. This wonderful exhibition is entertaining Chicagoans and visitors from June 1 through October 13, 2001.

This beautiful and whimsical exhibition of suites of furniture is only one of our city's many public art attractions. *Suite Home Chicago*® demonstrates that art does not have to be either "serious" or "hands off" for it to be effective and moving. Enjoy them through the summer and into October. When the exhibition closes on October 13, many of them are auctioned off to support charitable organizations.

Once again, thank you for supporting this excellent exhibition.

Sincerely,

Richard M. Daley, Mayor

Suite Home Chicago Comitee

Artists of Windy City Arts

"Public art projects like this not only generate fun and excitement for Chicagoans and visitors alike, they showcase the talent and diversity of Chicago's art community. *Suite Home Chicago®* is first and foremost a celebration of Chicago artists."

Richard M. Daley, Mayor, City of Chicago

The hallow atmosphere within a museum's walls might seem for many a far cry from the irreverence of the bustling city streets, but often it is the street where a Chicagoan's first engagement with fine art takes place: The ten-year-old girl who notices the faint lyrical sounds that emanate from Harry Bertoia's Untitled Sounding Sculpture while she waits for her friends to go ice skating in Grant Park; the defiant young skateboarder attempting to make a perfect jump off the slope of the base of the untitled work by Pablo Picasso in Daley Plaza, who pauses after his fourth or fifth or fiftieth try and, looking up, detects the genius of the Cubist form; the couple meeting for a date at Marc Chagall's mosaic, The Four Seasons, in Bank One Plaza and sees the joy of their lives reflected in the artist's celebratory composition.

These are the moments in which any member of the public becomes aware of the principles of art appreciation: taking the time to reflect on how an artist's expression makes a statement relevant to one's own life or, on a broader stage, the world at large. All too often, however, the rate at which many of us move through an increasingly complex world in order to negotiate our increasingly complicated lives makes such moments of contemplation somewhat rare.

It is in this environment that public-art projects such as *Suite Home Chicago®: An International Exhibition of Urban Street Furniture,* with its large-scale, vibrantly decorated objects that shout out to the public, beckon individuals to stop and sit (in this case literally) and think about the things and ideas with which they are confronted. This type of public project creates an event in which a great many dialogues can begin: that between the city and its citizens, between the organizers of the city's public and private sectors, and, probably most importantly, between objects and viewers, who begin to arbitrate for themselves and among one another the basis by which artistic expression may be valued.

Continued on page 42

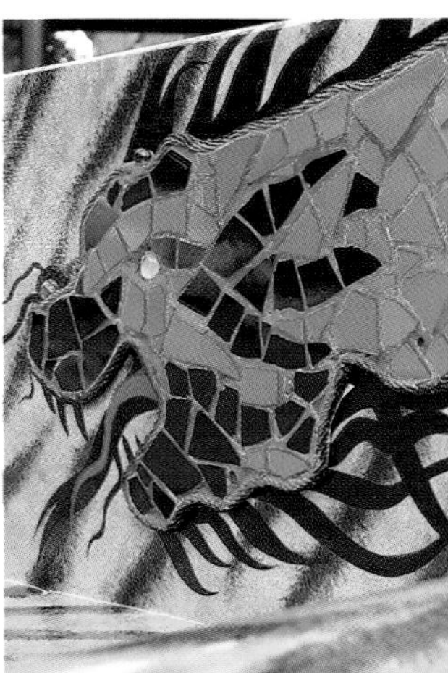

1 Couching Tiger, Hidden Dragon
21 E. Bellevue
Artist: Edrice Sirles
Sponsor: The Sutton Place Hotel

2 Black and White and Read All Over
60 W. Walton
Artists: Susan Mart, Frances Cox,
Ellen Roth Deutsch, Beverly Kedzior,
Marilynn Weitzmann, Jan Calek,
Marilyn Schulenberg
Sponsor: Newberry Library

Home on the Range
940 N. Michigan
Artist: Scott Piper, Exo Company and Skyline Design
Sponsor: LaSalle National Bank

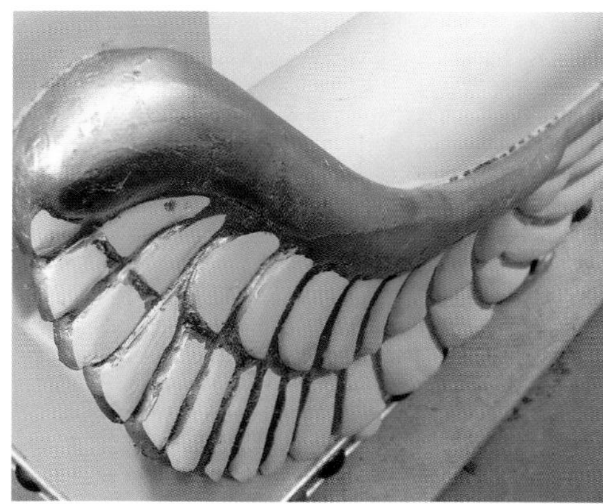

1 1 2
2

1 Egyptian Chair
112 E. Oak
Artist: Niedermaier Design Team
Sponsor: Marilyn Miglin, L.P.

2 Residential Transitions
980 N. Michigan
Artist: Jackie Moses
Sponsor: Rubloff Residential Properties

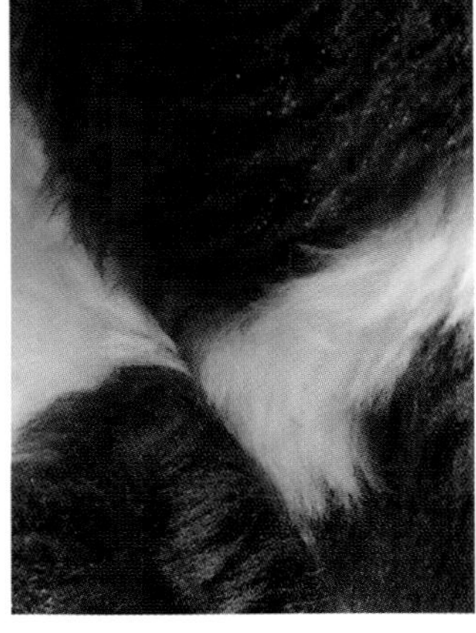

1 2
1 2

1 MozPod
980 N. Michigan
Artist: Jordan Mozer
Sponsor: Jordan Mozer & Associates, Ltd.

2 Phony Pony
100 E. Walton
Artist: Claire Ashley
Sponsor: The Morson Collection

1 2 2
1 3
3

1 Cat Nap
935 N. Michigan
Artist: Tiffany Stronsky
Sponsor: Drake Hotel

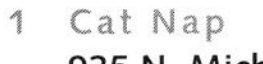

2 Chicago's Cows Come Home Suite Home
900 N. Michigan
Artist: Carol Stitzer
Sponsor: Interfaith House

3 Pick Up Your Clothes
920 N. Michigan
Artist: Nancy Gardner and Burt Isenstein
Sponsor: Mark Shale

Summer
900 N. Michigan
Artist: Mackenzie Thorpe
Sponsor: Atlas Galleries

Dawn in Porto San Giorgio, Italy
909 N. Michigan
Artist: Tom McGeary
Sponsor: Westin Michigan Avenue

1 1
1 2
2

1 Seat of Inspiration
105 E. Delaware
Artist: Ellen Gradman
Sponsor: The Whitehall Hotel

2 Bach-a-lounger
866 N. Michigan
Artist: Jane Perkins
Sponsor: Women's Board of the Ravinia Festival

1 2
1

1 Hot Rooms, Cold Sofa
862 N. Michigan
Artist: Colin Lambeides
Sponsor: Hot Rooms Division of Hotel Reservation Management Co.

2 MozPod
875 N. Michigan
Artist: Jordan Mozer
Sponsor: Jordan Mozer & Associates, Ltd.

Chicago's Suite Sisters
875 N. Michigan
Artist: Maryanne Warton, Sisters Too, Inc.
Sponsor: United Airlines

Hot Dog With Everything
840 N. Michigan
Artist: Paul Meyer
Sponsor: Chicago Magazine

Our Every Tree
The Illinois Shore / Tele-Vision
163 E. Pearson
Artist: Renee McGinnis
Sponsor: Chicago Office of Tourism

Hiz and Miz Honor
Water Tower Park, north side
of Historic Water Tower
Artist: Flair Communications Agency,
Maria Tubay and Stan Sczepanski;
Rick Tuttle and Kaleidoscope
Sponsor: Flair Communications Agency

1 Prime Time
875 N. Michigan
Artist: Jill Ricci
Sponsor: The Saloon Steakhouse

2 The Great White Long-legged Winged Homing Chair. Appears Only Once Every 5000 Years.
Historic Water Tower, 806 N. Michigan, south roof
Artist: Victor Skrebneski
Sponsor: Judy Niedermaier

1 2
1

1 Something from Nothing
50 E. Chicago
Artist: Student artists of Marwen
Sponsor: Lakewest, Inc.

2 Wishes Do Come True
111 E. Chicago
Artist: Shane McCall
Sponsor: American Girl Place

Suite Chicago Dogs
750 N. Michigan
Artist: Anne Leuck Feldhaus
Sponsor: HomeLife Furniture

Soda Fountain "Suite"
757 N. Michigan
Artist: JoAnne Conroy
Sponsor: Walgreens

1
1 2
2

1 Eli's Chairy Cheesecake
215 E. Chicago
Artist: Becky Flory and
Betty Lark Ross
Sponsor: The Eli's Cheesecake
Company

2 Untitled
220 E. Chicago
Artist: Patrick Miceli
Sponsor: Museum of
Contemporary Art

1 1 2
2

1 Talking Heads
744 N. Michigan
Artist: Patti Shapiro
Sponsor: Cole Taylor Bank

2 Life as Dance
730 N. Michigan
Artist: Zhou Brothers
Sponsor: The Peninsula Chicago

1 **High Chair**
720 N. Michigan
Artist: Victor Skrebneski
Sponsor: Saks Fifth Avenue

2 **Our Hometown**
700 N. Michigan
Artist: Maryanne Warton, Sisters Too, Inc.
Sponsor: Corrugated Supplies Corporation

1 2
2
2

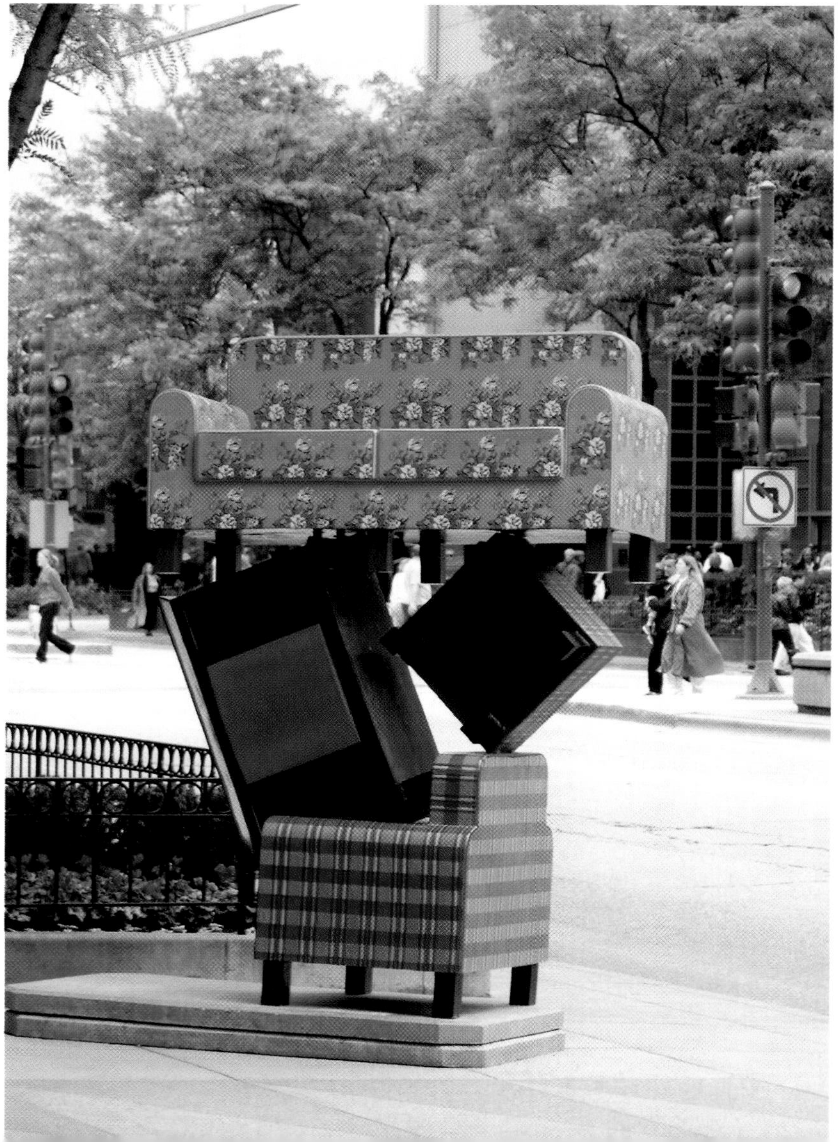

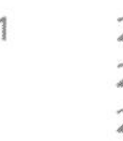

1 Moving Day
710 N. Michigan
Artist: J.C. Steinbrunner
Sponsor: Room & Board

2 Seat of Knowledge
660 N. Michigan
Artist: Mary Burke
Sponsor: Shimer College

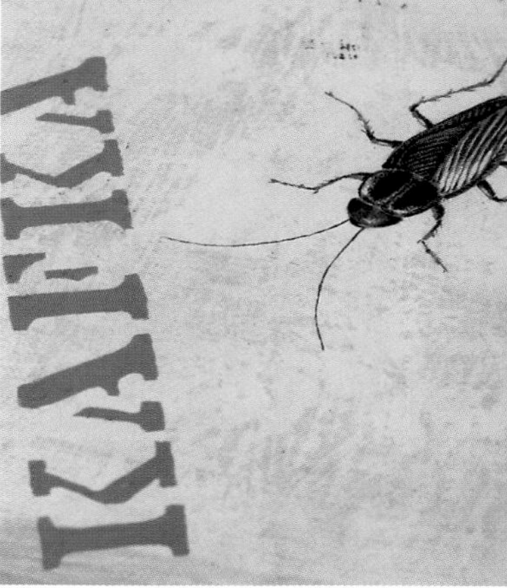

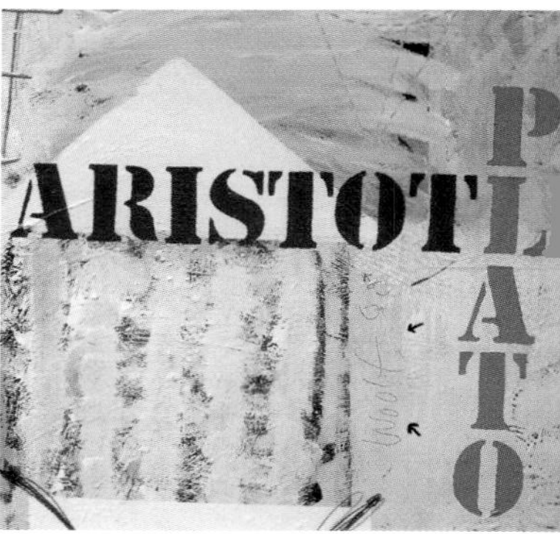

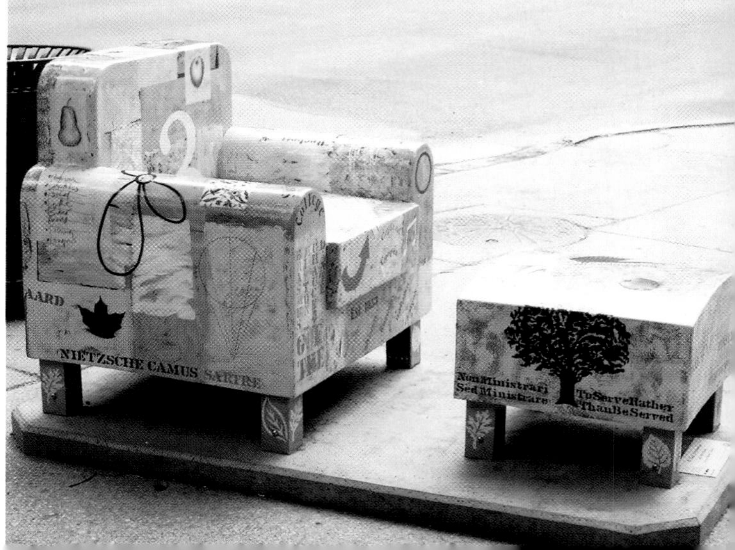

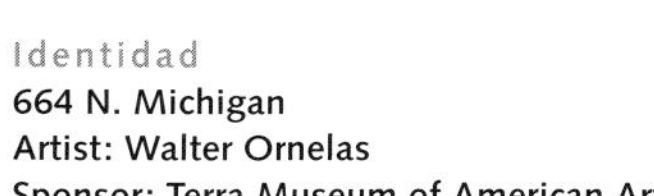

Identidad
664 N. Michigan
Artist: Walter Ornelas
Sponsor: Terra Museum of American Art

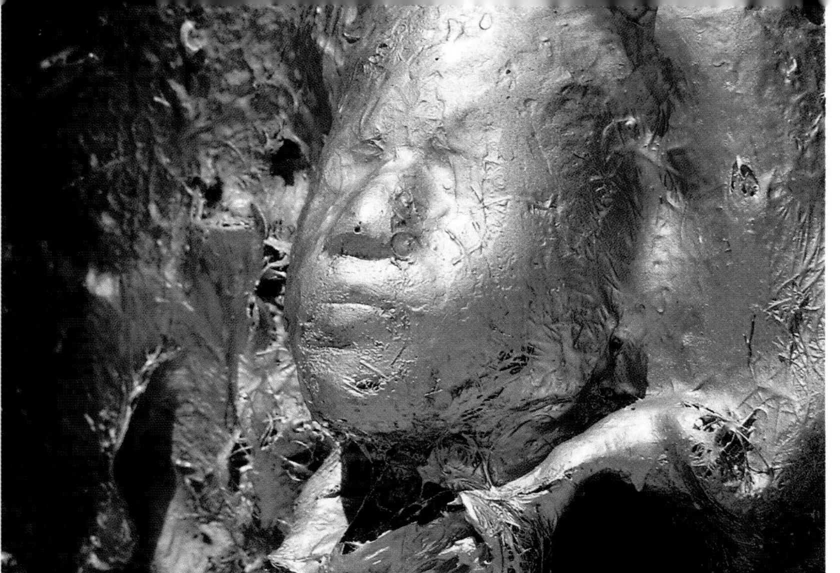

Cowch
660 N. Michigan
Artist: Dennis Callahan
Sponsor: Hanig's Footwear

The Casting Couch
663 N. Michigan
Artist: Michael Kutza
Sponsor: Chicago International Film Festival

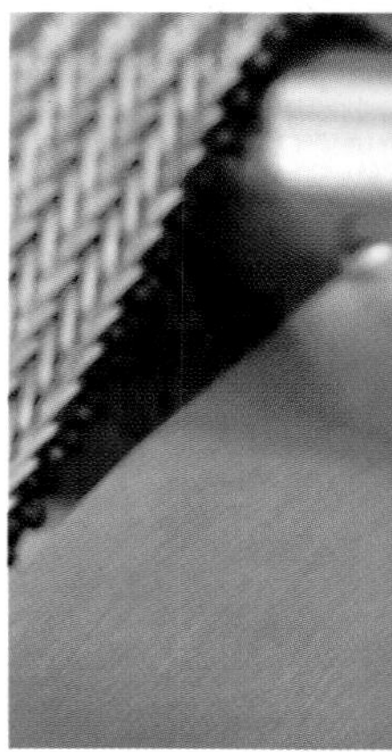

1 1
1 2
1 2

1 Windy City, Starry Night
671 N. Michigan
Artist: York Community High School
Sponsor: James McHugh Construction Co.

2 Sling Chair and Ottoman
665 N. Michigan
Artist: James Geier
Sponsor: 555 Design Fabrication Management, Inc.

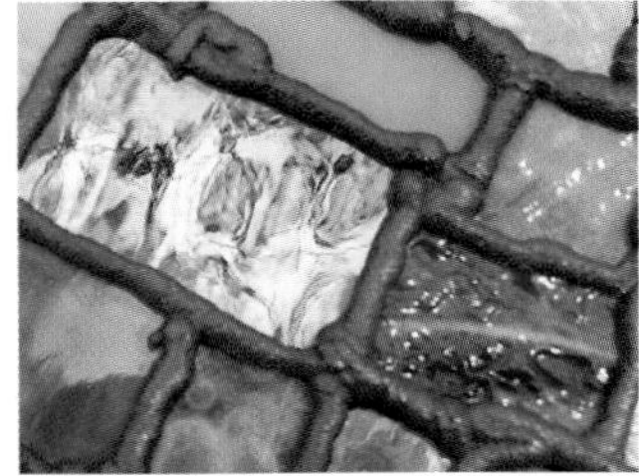

1 2
2
1

1 MON DIVAN
645 N. Michigan
Artist: Victor Skrebneski
Sponsor: Salvatore Ferragamo

2 Televisionary Art
646 N. Michigan
Artist: Jeffrey Conroy
Sponsor: FCB Chicago / True North

1 1
2 2

1 A Classic Combination
646 N. Michigan
Artist: Clayton Dibble and Laura Chamberlain
Sponsor: Crate & Barrel

2 Sitting Pretty
638 N. Michigan
Artist: Jeffrey Conroy
Sponsor: The Meeting Group, Inc.

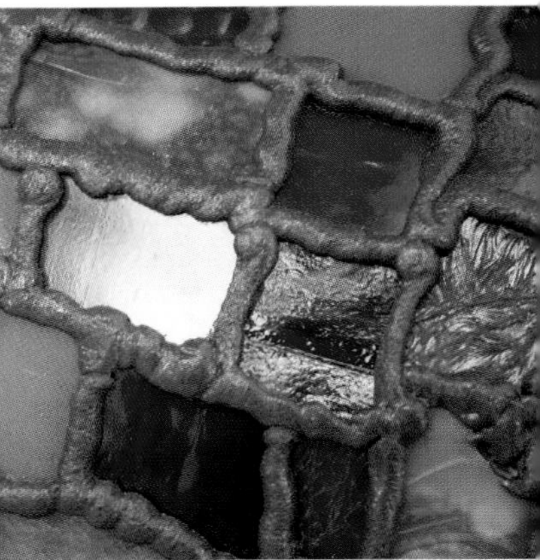

soFA, so good
638 N. Michigan
Artist: Jeffrey Conroy
Sponsor: Higgins Development Partners, LLC.

Town, Country, City
633 N. Michigan
Artist: Michael Dopp
Sponsor: Andrea Atlass and
Ken Kuehnle

Charity in the Neighborhood of our Success
625 N. Michigan
Artist: Jenny Steinman, Steinman Studios
Sponsor: Greater North Michigan Avenue
Association and Golub & Co.

1 1
1
2 2

1 Chicago Free Press:
Portraits of the Community
630 N. Michigan
Artist: Jason Smith
Sponsor: Chicago House and
Social Service Agency

2 El sillôn de la sabidurîa
620 N. Michigan
Artist: Alberto Senior
Sponsor: Lapiz

Deluxe Suite/Fabulous View
600 N. Michigan
Artist: S. Thom Cicchelli
Sponsor: Healthcare Information Management Systems Society

Continued from page 9

In 1965 President Lyndon B. Johnson sought to partner with the country's private patrons of the arts and culture with the establishment of his domestic program, Great Society. The intent of the program was that government-sponsored initiatives would improve the quality of life for all Americans – positing the idea that government can nurture the notion of value in the national psyche. In addition to substantial funds for social programs, Congress saw fit to support additional programs in education and the arts.

A short two years later, Chicago Mayor Richard J. Daley dedicated the city's first non-commemorative public monument, an untitled piece of Modern sculpture, now known internationally as the Picasso, in the then Civic Center Plaza across from his office at City Hall. The flurry of public opinion regarding the sculpture – including Pulitzer Prize winning newspaper columnist Mike Royko's declaration that the piece is nothing but a "big homely metal thing" – opened what might likely be termed the most democratic dialogue about fine art ever mounted. Since its dedication, the Picasso has not only come to be beloved by the larger part of Chicago's citizenry, but the controversy of its installation draws comparison to the Eiffel Tower of Paris, the other beloved monument that initially drew scorn from its local constituency. Thus, the Picasso is much cited as a success in fostering civic pride and, ultimately, a sense of ownership by the public of its shared space.

In the ensuing years, Chicago came to see its streets and plazas become a gallery for new works of large-scale art as pieces by Alexander Calder, Claes Oldenburg, and Isamu Noguchi were commissioned and installed in and around the central business district. In 1978, the city council approved an ordinance that made Chicago one of the first cities to reserve a percentage of the cost of constructing and renovating municipal buildings for the purchase of public art. The ordinance further stipulated that half the commissions be given to members of the local art community, furthering the idea that the work of artists who make the city their home shines as brightly as pieces by artists of foreign origin. As a result commissions by Roger Brown and Richard Hunt joined those by Richard Serra and Henry Moore.

In addition to large-scale works with budgets to match, the percent-for-art ordinance required artists to create objects for neighborhood schools and libraries. To fulfill this need, the Chicago Public Art Program – the agency created to administrate the commission of new and restoration of existing public art – began an artist slide registry. This catalogue of city residents who make their living or are trained as artists is a growing reference for city administrators to track artists whose expressions are influenced by life in Chicago and therefore relevant to local projects. The number of artists listed in this registry makes clear how many Chicagoans believe art and artistic expression lend significant meaning to their daily lives.

While the city reached out to its local community of artists, providing a greater number of venues for art objects to find viewers through the 1980s, private interests in the art market surged. Similarly, institutions such as museums and universities expanded programming – fine-art departments specializing in both practice and theory, art-education departments, new galleries for the examination and presentation of both trained and self-taught art, as well as time arts, installation, and new media – creating a virtual cottage industry based on artistic expression. Despite fluctuations in the economy, these programs continue to provide jobs and the ensuing tax base that is an integral part of any successful commercial enterprise.

It is in this environment that the fanciful idea for 1999's *Cows on Parade*™ became a phenomenon that captured the fancy of the city – and ultimately the nation, propagating a host of imitations in cities and towns across the country. *Cows on Parade*™, the American appropriation of Zurich, Switzerland's 1998 *Cow Parade*™, was suggested as a commercially sponsored exhibition by Chicago businessman Peter Hanig who became infatuated with the pageant of whimsically decorated cows he encountered on a family vacation in Europe.

Continued on page 82

Creativision
605 N. Michigan
Artist: Mr. Imagination
Sponsor: Intuit: The Center for Intuitive and Outsider Art

Stadium Seating
545 N. Michigan
Artist: John Llewellyn
Sponsor: Museum of Science and Industry and FireWorks for Kids Foundation

City Sunflower Garden
209 E. Ohio
Artist: Kate Tully
Sponsor: City Scents Flowers & Gifts

Zone Throne
43 E. Ohio
Artist: Dennis Callahan
Sponsor: ESPN Zone

1 1
2 2

1 Easy Living
55 E. Grand (Lobby)
Artist: Ruben Toledo
Sponsor: Nordstrom

2 Lazy Girl
520 N. Michigan
Artist: Ruben Toledo
Sponsor: Nordstrom

Anita's Flower Bed
535 N. Michigan
Artist: Michael Cheney
Sponsor: Atlas Galleries

1 Creature Comforts
161 E. Grand
Artist: Marko Markewycz
Sponsor: Opt1mus

2 Making an Impression
520 N. Michigan
Artist: Sheri Meketa/Hilligoss Galleries
Sponsor: The John Buck Co., The Shops at North Bridge

Nightlight Love Seat
520 N. Michigan
Artist: Randy Pijoan / Hilligoss Galleries
Sponsor: The John Buck Co., The Shops at North Bridge

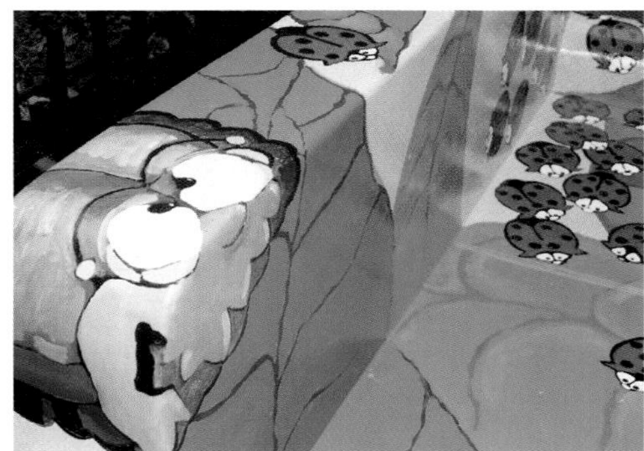

1 1 2
2

1 Lady Bug Invasion
510 N. Michigan
Artist: Arlena Tucker-Hampton
Sponsor: H.D. Hudson Manufacturing Company

2 Scenic Chicago
505 N. Michigan
Artist: Donna Antkowiak
Sponsor: Hotel Inter-Continental

Chicago's Suite Seasonal Bodies
500 N. Michigan
Artist: Lois Hrejsa
Sponsor: Day's Inn Lincoln Park North

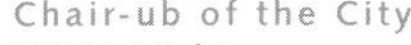

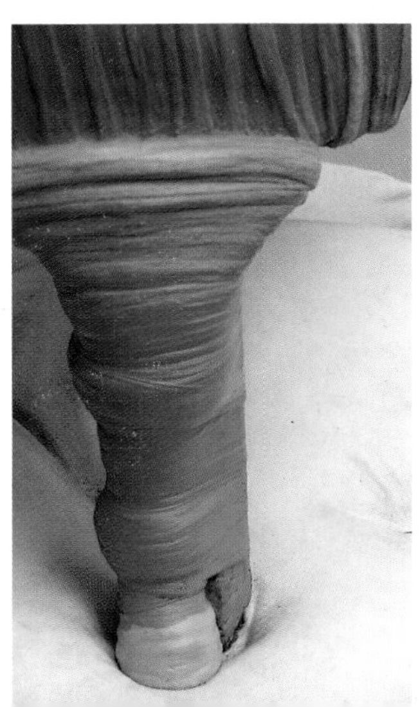

Chair-ub of the City
500 N. Michigan
Artist: Constance Lee Trojnar-Gauba
Sponsor: Avenue Business Center

Bungalow Belt
444 N. Michigan
Artist: Robert Gadomski
Sponsor: Toms-Price Home Furnishings, Wheaton and Lincolnshire

1 1 2
1
2
2

1 Chicago's Talking Heads
430 N. Michigan
Artist: Studio 676
Sponsor: Manning Selvage & Lee

2 Everyday People
420 N. Michigan
Artist: Apache Wakefield
Sponsor: Andrea Atlass and Ken Kuehnle

Spring is in the Air
410 N. Michigan
Artist: Vesna Lazar
Sponsor: Vesna Lazar

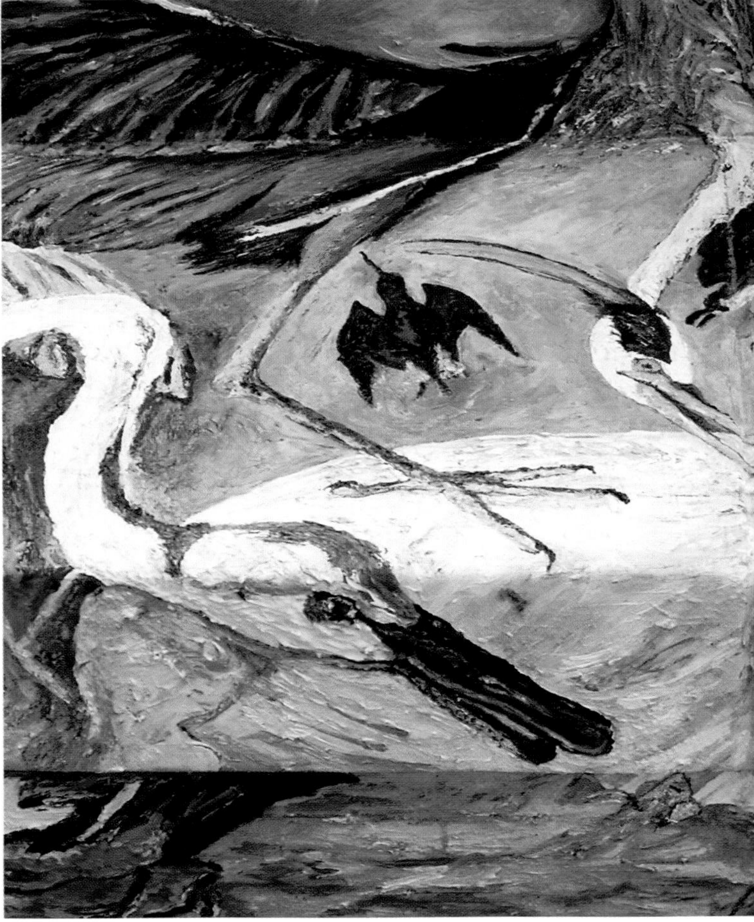

Sanctuary
410 N. Michigan
Artist: Michelle Stone
Sponsor: Kenyon Oppenheimer, Inc.

A Room With A View
400 N. Michigan
Artist: Kelly Rauch, Rauch Studio
Sponsor: American Liver Foundation, Illinois Chapter

Famous Faces, Chicago Places
400 N. Michigan
Artist: Mitch O'Connell
Sponsor: William Wrigley Jr.
Company Foundation

Don't Just Sit There –
Do Something
400 N. Michigan
Artist: BBDO Chicago
Sponsor: Illinois Bureau of Tourism

Cowgirl
400 N. Michigan
Artist: Jared Joslin
Sponsor: Sotheby's

The Fabric of a Whole New Sky
400 N. Michigan
Artist: Glenn Harris
Sponsor: Singapore Airlines

1 **Sunday Morning**
435 N. Michigan
Artist: Dennis Callahan and MARC USA / Chicago
Sponsor: Chicago Tribune

1 **Lava 36**
401 N. Michigan
Artist: George Mac and Steven Jackson
Sponsor: Haggerty Enterprises, Inc.

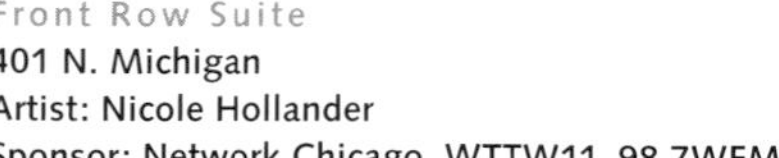

Front Row Suite
401 N. Michigan
Artist: Nicole Hollander
Sponsor: Network Chicago, WTTW11, 98.7WFMT, CityTalk

Love Suite
401 N. Michigan
Artist: Georgan Damore
Sponsor: IKEA

Fourniture
401 N. Michigan
Artist: Kozan Studios
Sponsor: ArtDogZ.com

Legroom
401 N. Michigan
Artist: Exhibit Group Giltspur
Sponsor: American Airlines

To Go
453 N. Cityfront Plaza
Artist: JoAnne Conroy
Sponsor: Clark/White Hen Pantry

Sweet Home Chicago
453 N. Cityfront Plaza
Artist: Youlia Tkatchouk
Sponsor: NBC 5

Deconstructive Dreams: Sebastian, Maximus, Simeon, Longinus
Columbus/Illinois
Artist: Jorge Cruz
Sponsor: Embassy Suites Hotel – Chicago Downtown Lakefront

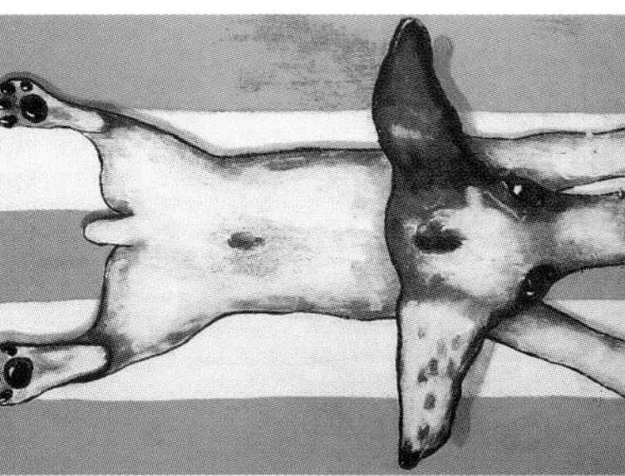

TV Funtime
Navy Pier
Artist: Lois Keller
Sponsor: Metropolitan Pier and Exposition Authority

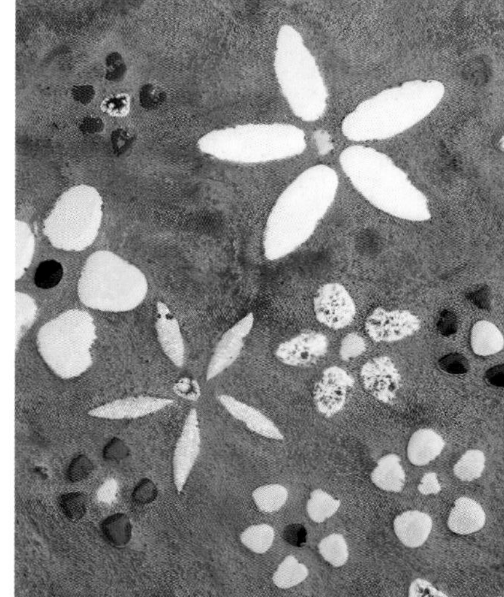

Spring, Summer, Fall, Winter
Navy Pier
Artist: Suzanne Rampage and Sara McLean
Sponsor: Metropolitan Pier and Exposition Authority

Haworth Suite: Furniture[3]
303 E. Wacker
Artist: The Environments Group
Sponsor: Chicago House and
Social Service Agency

Chicago's Future Furniture Suite
151 E. Wacker
Artist: Allan Hicks
Sponsor: Hyatt Regency Chicago

Glass Bottom Sofa
Michigan / Wacker (on the dock)
Artist: Maryanne Warton,
Sisters Too, Inc.
Sponsor: Chicago's First Lady

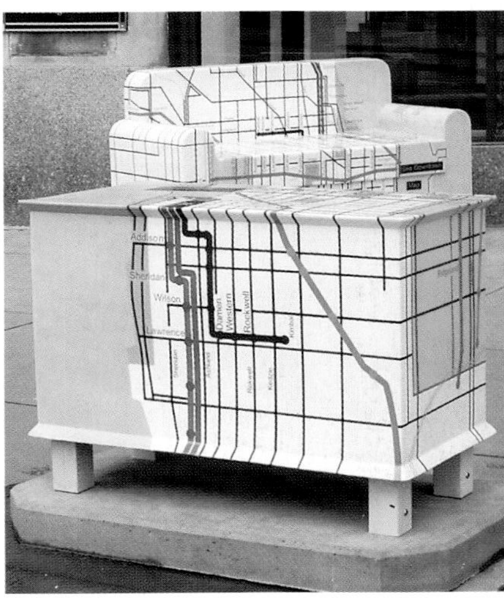

1 1 2
1
2

1 Haworth Suite: REST
Michigan / Wacker
(northeast corner)
Artist: Gary Lee Partners
Sponsor: Chicago House and
Social Service Agency

2 Suite Home Chicago, a set
360 N. Michigan
Artist: Plamen Yordanov
Sponsor: Microsoft Corporation

Windy City Sofa
Michigan / Wacker (northwest corner)
Artist: Joyce Polance
Sponsor: Chicago Sun-Times

1 2 2
2

1 Homage to Sergei Eisenstein
200 N. Michigan
Artist: John Conklin
Sponsor: Chicago Opera Theatre

2 Harmonious Diversity
200 N. Michigan
Artist: Rashid Moussouni
Sponsor: Chicago Association of Realtors

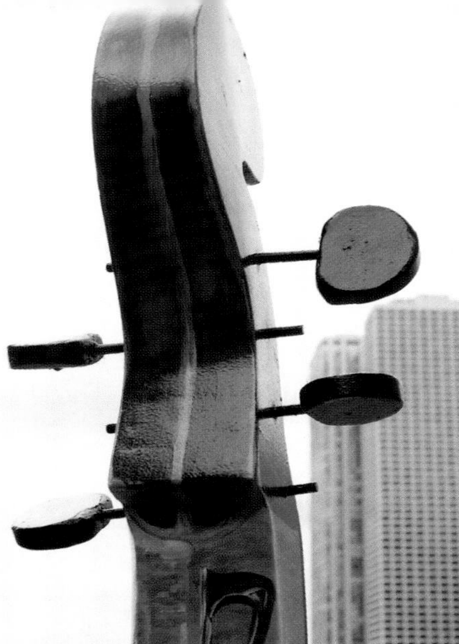

First Chair
200 N. Columbus
Artist: BettyAnn Mocek
Sponsor: Fairmont Chicago

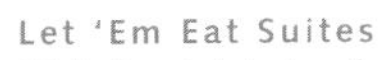

Let 'Em Eat Suites
66 E. Randolph, (roof garden)
Artist: Gallery 37
Apprentice Artists
Sponsor: Arts Matter Foundation

Continued from page 43

In the short nine months that *Cows on Parade*™ went from idea to implementation, it morphed into a hybrid spectacle: a public-art event. The partnership between the public and private sectors was an unusually equitable exploitation of the expertise each faction brought to the project: Commercial enterprise with its marketing savvy could outline and sell a sponsorship structure for the event at a fair market value. The variety of sponsors were then able to bring public attention to the project by the sheer number of behind-the-scenes participants. Similarly, the city was able to galvanize the community of local artists not only to create objects for the exposition, but to staff the operation required to mount and maintain it.

Almost as soon as it was unveiled, the public became enamoured with the project. Its greatest conceptual success seemed to be its ability to cause viewers to pause and reflect on seemingly out of place objects. Whether they were merely evaluating the success of the various versions of decoration or contemplating notions of propriety, irony, and/or eccentricity, the event provided almost continuous opportunities for viewers to participate in either serious or superficial dialogues. Both print and broadcast media garnered further viewer response, including a forum of reactions to the exhibit on metromix.com and a regular feature in the *Chicago Sun-Times* titled, "What's Your Favorite Cow." The growing amount of press spread word of the event beyond the city limits, creating a rise in tourism and an economic impact estimated to be as much as $200 million. The event culminated in an auction that raised nearly $3.5 million for local charities. With this success, the city was reminded of an important lesson in marketing: Accessibility gives rise to acceptance. If just one person is better able to comprehend the abstract expression of Calder's Flamingo in Federal Center Plaza as a result of examining the success (or lack thereof) of a single fiberglass cow, the event will have succeeded in a way far more profound than its fiscal outcome.

Despite this lofty effect, however, economic success is a great instigator in a capital culture. The success of *Cows on Parade*™, as well as the lessons learned from it, necessitated a sequel. The trick – the onus placed on the staff of the Department of Cultural Affairs – was to ensure a follow-up event that took the lessons learned from its predecessor and become an event with its own identity rather than a pale comparison of the original.

During the summer of 2001, Chicago residents and visitors to the city were confronted by *Suite Home Chicago*®, a collection of fiberglass sofas, chairs, ottomans and TV consoles presented individually and in groupings designed and decorated by Chicago artists, artisans, and designers. The success of *Cows on Parade*™ secured the participation of a host of Chicago businesses anxious to participate in another public-art spectacle. Primary among these is Niedermaier, a Chicago furniture manufacturer, which designed all the fiberglass forms for the project. From the onset, *Suite Home Chicago*® was organized as a project that would spread the earnings of its success to as many local entities as possible. The selection of furniture as the objects to be put on display was difficult in light of the ebullient reception received by the cows of *Cows on Parade*™. Clearly it would be foolish to attempt to duplicate the sense of affability the public instilled in the anthropomorphized pieces of the first event. For the second outing the organizers had to identify objects with a similar universal affinity without relying so heavily on sheer charm. This edict alone ensured the experience the public would have with the works comprising the sequel would be more serious in tone, bringing the public closer to the dialogues of fine art. Furniture was identified as a product with which the city has a long-standing history of design, production, and commerce.

Simultaneous with *Suite Home Chicago®*, the exhibit *Beyond Function: The Art of Furniture,* displayed forty-three pieces of handmade furniture and objects by 39 local designers at the Chicago Cultural Center. Showcasing the creative solutions and artistry these artisans bring to their professional practice, "Beyond Function" was labeled as a response by the furniture-making community to the bravado of *Suite Home Chicago®*. In this case the public-art event provided the opportunity for a professional organization – the Chicago Furniture Designers Association – to spotlight the more serious or pragmatic concerns of the industry to which the objects in the public-art event allude. In addition to the exhibition of furniture, "Beyond Function" included text, photographs, or video that describe the intentions of the designers along with the evolution of the design from the initial concept, sketch, and model to the finished object.

Consensus indicates few people regard the decorated fiberglass forms of *Suite Home Chicago®* as objects of high art. Rather, they are similar to art cars, the decorated vehicles one sees parked on the street or driving up the road that cause one to stop and think: Who made that car? Why was it made? What is it trying to represent? Regardless of the true artistic value such objects manifest, they successfully accomplish one of the goals of all the arts: to elicit a reaction; to make people think.

1 1 1
2

1 Fusion
224 S. Michigan
Aritst: Interior Architecture Studio
Sponsor: Skidmore,
Owings & Merrill, LLP

2 Stand BY Seating
Replacement Suite
Artist: Sergio Roca
Sponsor: Chicago Department
of Cultural Affairs

Peep Hole
Chicago Cultural Center
78 E. Washington
Artist: Cabell and Stephanie Heyward
Sponsor: Arts Council of Beaufort County, South Carolina

Paint the Town
540 N. Michigan
Artist: Vincent Rincon
Sponsor: Chicago Marriott Downtown

1 1 2

1 Consumption I and II
Chicago Cultural Center
77 E. Randolph
Artist: Yollocalli Youth Museum
Sponsor: Chicago Transit Authority

2 Vegetable: Cause and Effect
40 S. Michigan
Artist: Adam Brooks
Sponsor: Gallery 312

Who's Watching who / Time
Chicago Cultural Center
77 E. Randolph, Inside Visitor Center
Artist: David Philpot
Sponsor: David Philpot

Kite Kouch
150 S. Michigan
Artist: Artists of Windy City Arts
Sponsor: Windy City Arts

Live It Up in Singapore!
200 S. Michigan
Artist: JoAnne Conroy and Aaron Goland
Sponsor: Singapore Tourism Board

Salute to the 'tute
200. S. Michigan
Artist: David Moose
Sponsor: Jim and Barbara Hanig

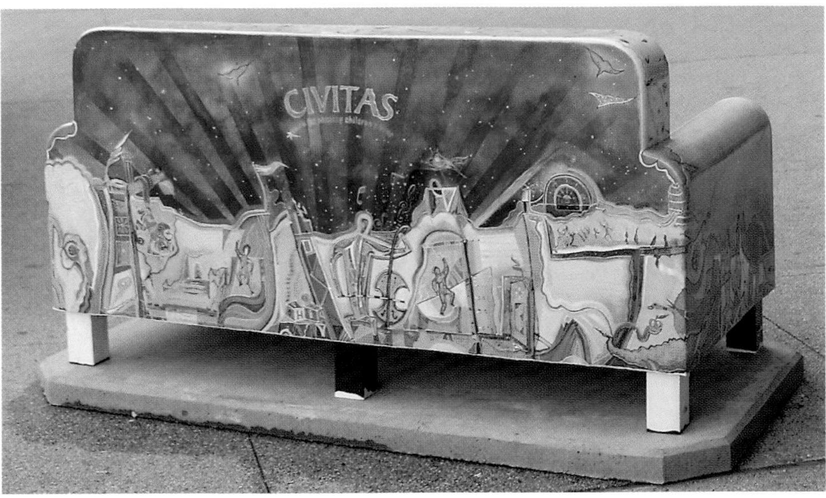

CHILD-SEAT
418 S. Michigan
Artist: gARTh
Sponsor: The Rizai Family

1 2

1 The Fireside Chat
430 S. Michigan
Artist: Zsofia Otvos
Sponsor: Roosevelt University

2 Leafy Lounger
Congress Plaza
Artist: Jennifer Graham Caswell
Sponsor: Jennifer Graham Caswell

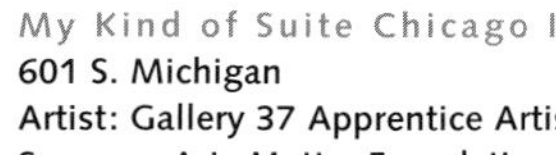

My Kind of Suite Chicago Is
601 S. Michigan
Artist: Gallery 37 Apprentice Artists
Sponsor: Arts Matter Foundation

Magnificent 4
905 S. Michigan
Artist: Gallery 37 Apprentice Artists
Sponsor: Arts Matter Foundation

People, Places & Neighborhood Spaces
Buckingham Fountain
Artist: Dennis Callahan
Sponsor: Chicago Department of Planning and Development

Sweet Suite
Buckingham Fountain
Artist: Jo Hormuth and Micki LeMieux
Sponsor: Sara Lee Foundation

1 Seat of Imagination, Chicago
401 S. State
Artist: 2-D Design Art-100 and Konrad F. Hack
Sponsor: Robert Morris College

2 Black & White in Color
Federal Plaza, 220 S. Dearborn
Artist: Jonathan Franklin and Student Artists
Sponsor: Art Resources in Teaching

River Suite
311 S. Wacker
Artist: Phil Schuster
Sponsor: 311 S. Wacker Building

Kaleido-couch
311 S. Wacker
Artist: Gallery 37, Apprentice Artists
Sponsor: Arts Matter Foundation

Metropolis 233
233 S. Wacker
Artist: BettyAnn Mocek
Sponsor: Sears TowerSkydeck / Trizec Hahn

1 1 2
1
2

1 Favorite Memories
500 W. Monroe
Artist: Artists of Renaissance Court
Sponsor: Heller Financial

2 A Seat on the Exchange
10 S. Wacker
Artist: Dawn Madison
Sponsor: Segall Bryant & Hamill Investment Counsel

Furniture by the Brook
110 S. LaSalle
Artist: Warren Hines and Diosdado Mondero
Sponsor: Brook Furniture Rental

"Tweet" Home Chicago
120 S. LaSalle
Artist: Gailene Cowger Fine and Betty Nicks
Sponsor: Baird and Warner

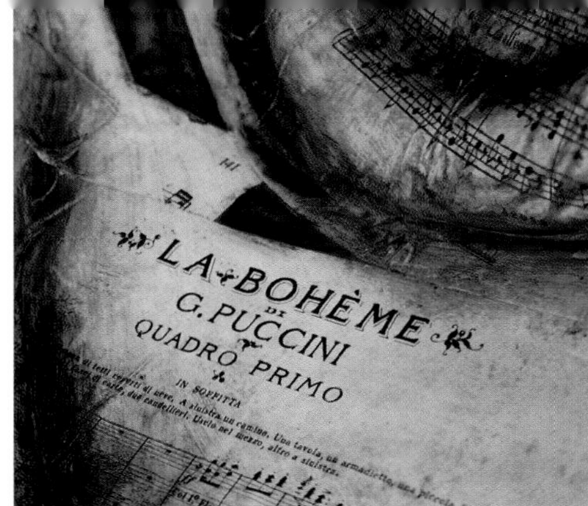

1
1 2 2
2

1 A-R-I-A going to take a seat?
20 N. Wacker
Artist: Scott Marr
Sponsor: Lyric Opera of Chicago

2 Cultivating Growth
111 W. Monroe
Artist: Chicago Botanic Garden Staff
Sponsor: Harris Bank

Springin'!
1 S. State (in planter)
Artist: Furniture by Carson Pirie Scott's Visual Team, Tea Tray by Linda Mueller
Sponsor: Carson Pirie Scott & Company

1 2 2

1 New Home Chicago
1 N. State
Artist: N. Eden Unluata
Sponsor: Lee Lumber

2 Untitled
10 S. Wabash
Artist: Darius Cyrlik
Sponsor: Crowne Plaza Chicago – The Silversmith

Blah, Blah, Blah
2 N. State
Artist: Sears CCM Design
Sponsor: Sears, Roebuck & Co.

Suite 37
100 N. State
Artist: Gallery 37
Apprentice Artists
Sponsor: Arts Matter Foundation

1 1 2
1
1
2

1 For the Douglas Transit Arts Program
Daley Plaza, 50 W. Washington
Artist: Little Black Pearl Workshop
Sponsor: Chicago Transit Authority

2 Seat of the World
Daley Plaza, 60 W. Washington
Artist: Margaret Graham Caswell
Sponsor: Margaret Graham Caswell

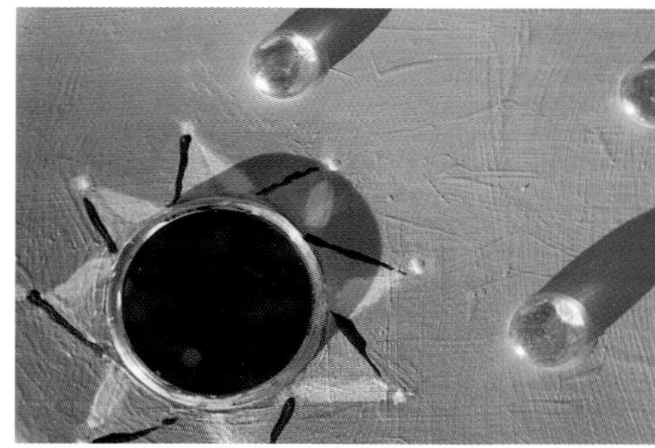

1 1
2 2

1 Untitled
171 W. Randolph
Artist: Engineering Staff
Sponsor: Hotel Allegro

2 "Claire's Hometown Blues,"
A Salute to Goodman Theatre
170 N. Dearborn
Artist: Mhorag Taylor, Trudi Goodman, Laura Olsen, Mark Bickford, Erin Duggan, Mary Hoffman
Sponsor: Ethan Allen and Benjamin Moore

Nutty-Popping at State and Lake
190 N. State
Artist: Estelle Kenney
Sponsor: Nuts on Clark

Sofa(r) from Home
100 W. Randolph (lobby)
Artist: Patients of Rush Children's Hospital with Instructors and Artists of Snow City Arts Foundation
Sponsor: Snow City Arts Foundation

Odalisque
111 N. State
Artist: KINC Chromize / Katherine Ross and Karen Zissis
Sponsor: Marshall Field's

Full Moon **(Picture right)**
111 N. State
Artist: Thomas O'Brien
Sponsor: Marshall Field's

Marshall Field's
Marshall Field's

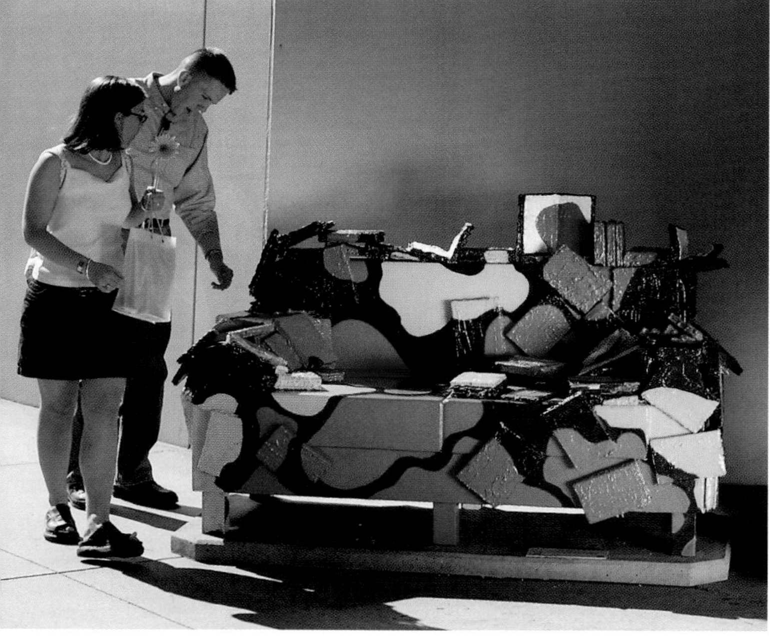

1 2 2
2
1

1 Read Awhile
30 E. Lake
Artist: Students and Faculty of Harold Washington College
Sponsor: Harold Washington College

2 At Home in the Windy City
225 W. Wacker
Artist: Ross Fiersten
Sponsor: Morningstar, Inc.

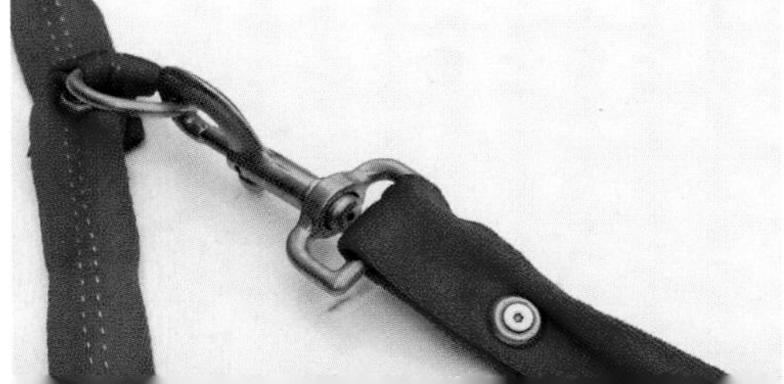

1 2
2

1 Kings of the Couch
Merchandise Mart
Artist: Glenn Wexler
Sponsor: Boise Cascade Office Products Corporation

2 Otto and Owner
Merchandise Mart
Artist: Gretchen Wustrack, IDEO
Sponsor: Steelcase, Inc. & Johnson Associates

1 2
1 2

1 City Scapes
Merchandise Mart (Lobby)
Artist: Sister Nagsters
Sponsor: Merchandise Mart Properties, Inc.

2 Mission Chair (20 feet tall)
Merchandise Mart (Lobby)
Artist: Gustav Stickley and Toms-Price Home Furnishings, Wheaton and Lincolnshire
Sponsor: Toms-Price Home Furnishings, Wheaton and Lincolnshire

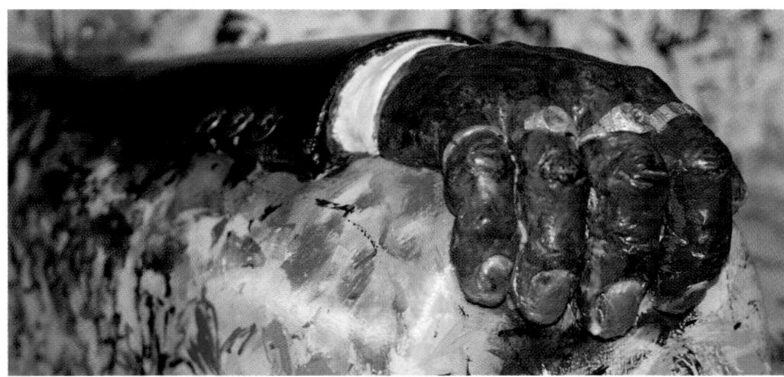

Jazz Roots
330 N. State
Artist: Kathryn Gauthier
Sponsor: House of Blues Hotel, A Loews Hotel

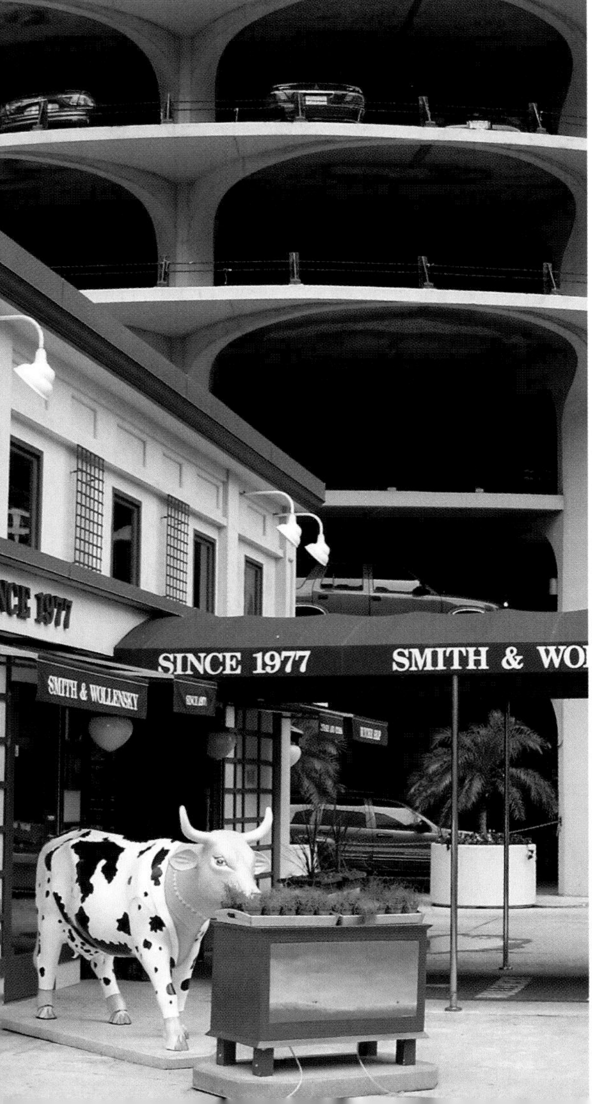

1 1 2
1
2

1 TV Dinner
318 N. State
Artist: Veronique Fontaine
Sponsor: Smith & Wollensky

2 Les Jardin de Metropolitan
IBM Plaza
Artist: Glenn Harris
Sponsor: Chicago Gateway Green Committee

1 1 2
2

1 Dialysis
215 W. Illinois
Artist: Patty Carroll
Sponsor: National Kidney Foundation of Illinois

2 Via Couchina
674 N. Wells
Artist: John T. Olson Decorators and deGiulio Kitchen Design
Sponsor: deGiulio Kitchen Design, Inc.

In Transit
426 W. Ohio
Artist: Boban Ilic
Sponsor: East Bank Storage Co.

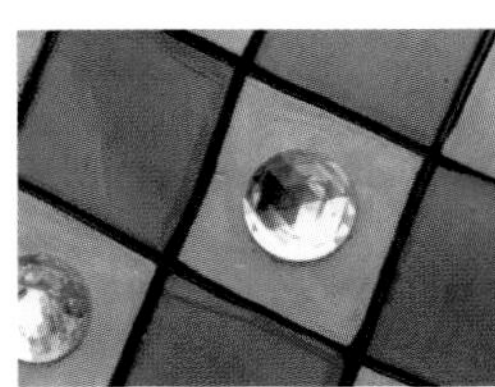

Indian Chair
111 W. Huron
Artist: Niedermaier Design Team
Sponsor: Wacker Apartments Hotel

1 1
2 2

1 Chicago in Black and White
1601 N. Clark
Artist: Jonathan Franklin
Sponsor: Chicago Historical Society

2 ColorWeave
850 W. North
Artist: April Head and
Tracy Rateike
Sponsor: Crate & Barrel

Eden's Living Room
Lincoln Park Conservatory, 2400 N. Stockton
Artist: Howard Blume, Sherae Patterson, Christopher Sasser, Michelle Loftin
Sponsor: Bay Furniture and Gethsemane Garden Center

1 "What Price Vanity," A Salute to Steppenwolf Theatre
1700 N. Halsted
Artist: Mark Bickford, Allison Schuch, Mary Hoffman
Sponsor: Ethan Allen and Benjamin Moore

2 Ottttttto the Millipede
Museum Campus: Idea Garden
Artist: Ion Cush
Sponsor: Public Art Conservation Endowment

1
2 2

1 Casting Couch
Lakefront, near water taxis
Artist: Patrick Knoll, Peter Taylor, Dennis Javier, Herbie Diaz
Sponsor: DDB Chicago and Skyline Design

2 As the World Turns
Adler Planetarium, 700 E. Solidarity
Artist: Ronit Mitchell and Scott Bullock, Penumbra Studio
Sponsor: Adler Planetarium & Astronomy Museum

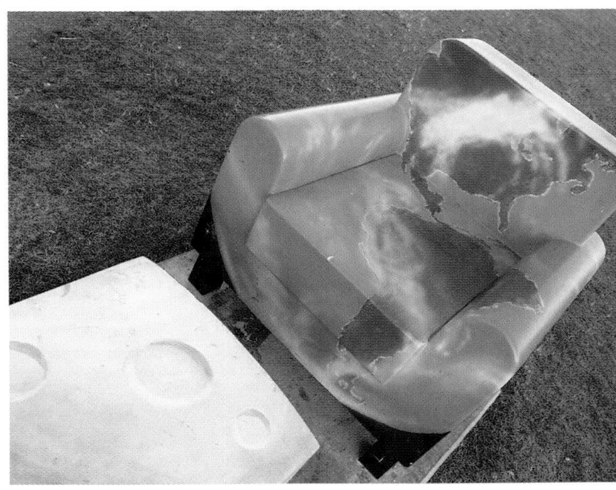

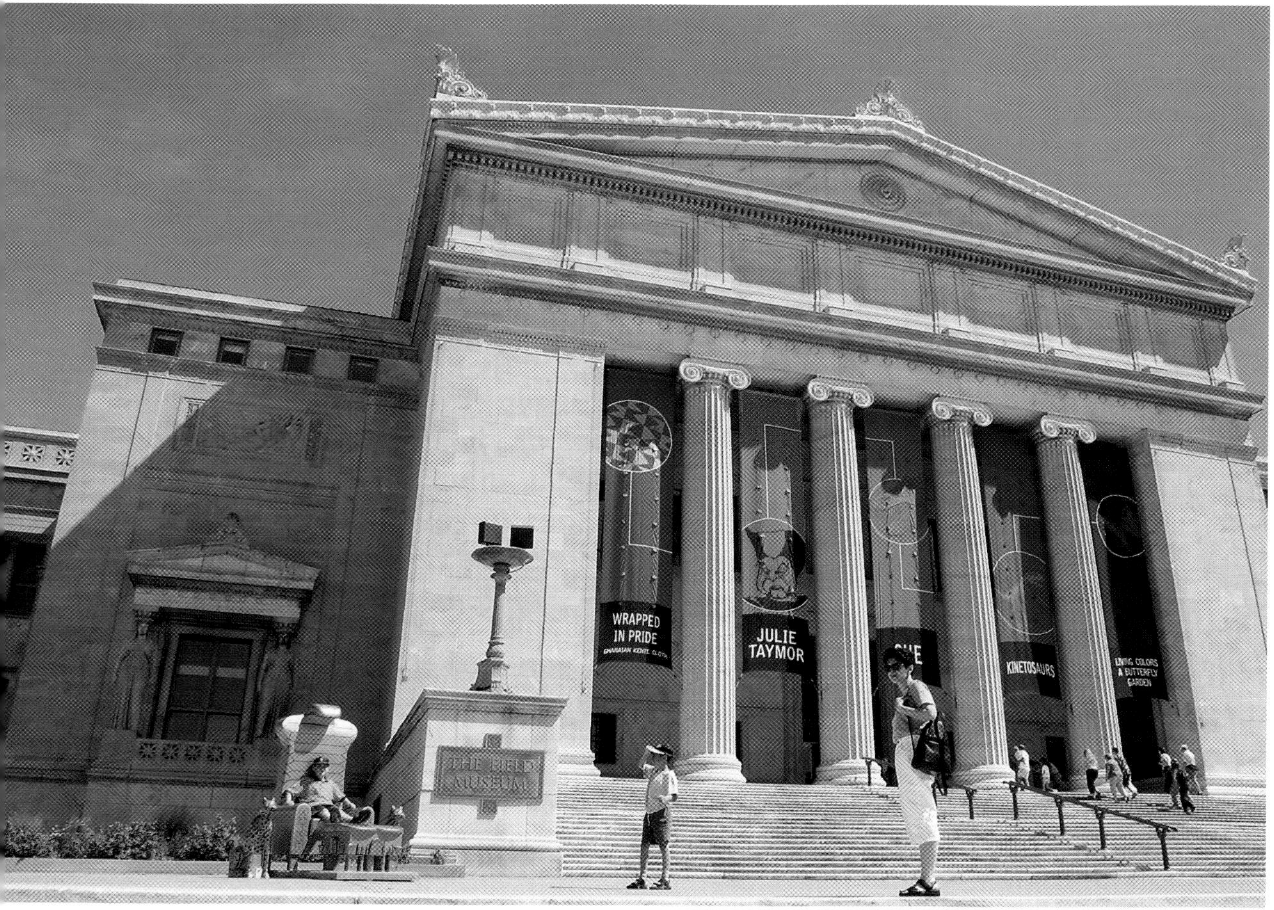

Cleopatra's Throne
The Field Museum, 1400 S. Lake Shore
Artist: David Hanke
Sponsor: The Field Museum

City in a Garden
The Field Museum, 1400 S. Lake Shore
Artist: Robert Klunk
Sponsor: Podmajersky Management, Inc.

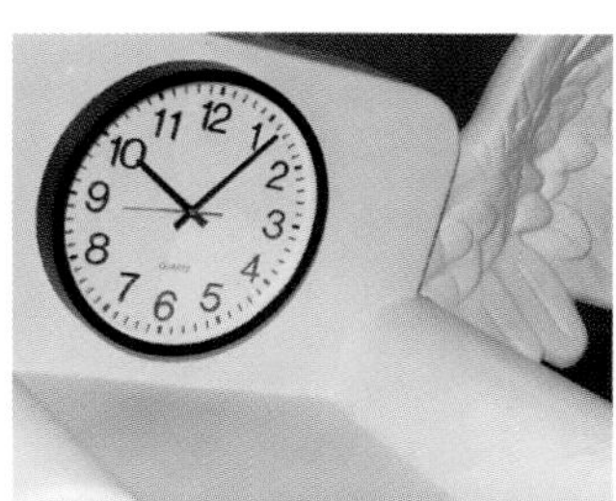

1
1 1 2
2

1 The Hollywood Davenporter
Museum of Science and Industry, 57th and Lake Shore Drive
Artist: John Llewellyn
Sponsor: Museum of Science and Industry

2 Time Flies
Museum of Science and Industry, 57th and Lake Shore Drive
Artist: Niedermaier Design Team
Sponsor: National Time Museum

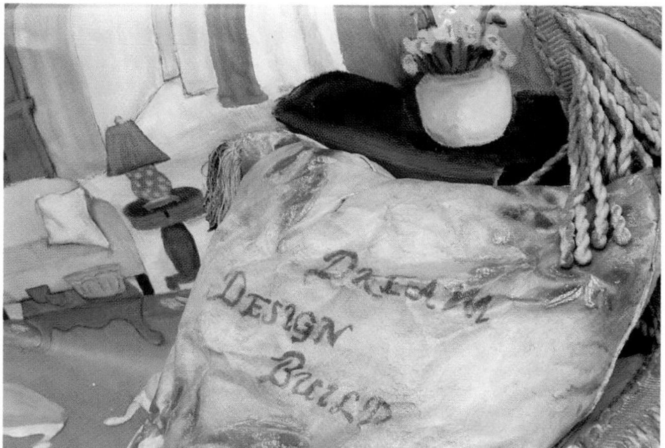

A Dream Come True
2009 N. Clybourn
Artist: Courtney Johnson
Sponsor: Walter E. Smithe Custom Furniture, Inc.

500 Lines of Resolution
Midway Airport, 5500 S. Cicero, Food Court
Artist: Aemiliano Jaure
Sponsor: Chicago Department of Aviation

Hands That Make Chicago Work
O'Hare Airport, Terminal 2
Artist: Kenn Alex Levesque
Sponsor: Chicago Department of Aviation

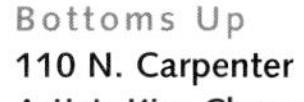

Bottoms Up
110 N. Carpenter
Artist: Kim Chong Ok Massey
Sponsor: Harpo Studios

1 1
2

1 Suite Leilani
Prudential Plaza
Artist: Steve Dahl
Sponsor: Steve Dahl & Company

2 What Goes Around Comes Around
320 N. Clark
Artist: Don Drabik, Amundsen Drabik
Sponsor: Friedman Properties

When Guys Dream
Circuiting the City on a Flatbed
Artist: Dennis Callahan
Sponsor: Circuit City

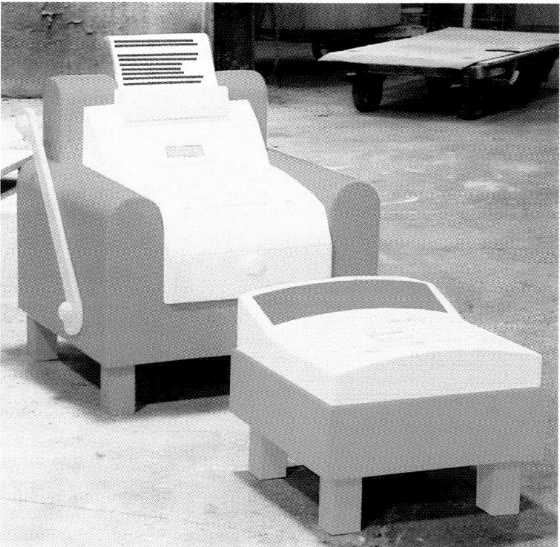

1
2
3
4

1 **Side Chair**
Water Tower Park
Artist: Victor Skrebneski
Sponsor: Hyatt Hotels of Chicago

2 **Mile Long Sofa**
Congress Plaza
Artist: Niedermaier Design Team
Sponsor: Niedermaier, Inc.

3 **Cash Couch**
2 S. LaSalle
Artist: Niedermaier Design Team
Sponsor: Manufacturers Bank

4 **Let's sit down and talk**
1 S. Wacker
Artist: Niedermaier Design Team
Sponsor: American Express Tax and Business Services

The artist index lists all of the artists in the exhibition with page numbers where their works are pictured. Works completed after the publication deadline were not photographed.

Suite Home Chicago® Committee

Daniel Nack, Chair-man
Carol Stitzer, Chair-woman
Edith Altman
Stevie Ball
Robert Bathon
Alexander L. Brown
Michael Christ
Paul Fairchild
Pete Fazio
Helyn Goldenberg
Gabrielle Griffin
Antoinette Haberkorn
Peter Hanig
Michael Heltzer
Rhona Hoffman
Tiffani Kim
Claire Wolf Krantz
Averill Leviton
Gary Metzner
Jenny Miller
Ellen Morse
Nina Newhouser
Judy Niedermaier
Julie Noh
Bill Noonan
Erica Pantuso
Russell Salzman
Sean Scott
Victor Skrebneski
Stan Sloan
Frank J. Uvena
Dana Waldman
Carter Williams
Michael Zartman

Major Underwriters:

Walgreens

Official Airline

Underwriters:

Sotheby's Chicago

Day's Inn Lincoln Park North
Official Hotel

The Chicago Department of Cultural Affairs is grateful to the following major underwrithers, who have generously donated their time and resources to his project.

Cows on Parade in Chicago
Author Mary Ellen Sullivan
Pictures Simon Koenig
Pages 180. Pictures 331. Cows 254.
ISBN 3-85923-042-X

COW Parade · Zurich's lighter Side
Author Walter Baumann
Pictures Marcel Werren
Pages 168. Pictures 332. Cows 289.
ISBN 3-85923-044-6

Art+Cow Salzburg 2000
Autor Dr. Karl Heinz Ritschel
Pictures Susanne Stadler
Pages 144 . Pictures 331. Cows 160
ISBN 3-85820-140-5

BenchArt Zurich 2001
Author Walter Baumann
Pictures ilka Michel
Pages 192 . Pictures 650. Benches 400
ISBN 3-85820-145-6

Unique:
Quality-COW-Watch
Made in Switzerland
Limited numbered edition of 999 ex.
ISBN 3-85820-123-5

To order:

Shop at the Cultural Center
78 E. Washington
Chicago, Illinois 60602
312.742.0079

Merchandise may also be purchased on the internet at www.chicagostore.com

NeptunArt · CH-8280 Kreuzlingen
E-mail: neptun@bluewin.ch · www.neptunart.ch